HOW THE CAT GOT HIS HAT:
THE STORY OF
Dr. Seuss

by Mark Spann

illustrated by
Barbara Kelley

MODERN CURRICULUM PRESS
Pearson Learning Group

T ed Geisel wandered down a New York
City street on a chilly day early in 1937.
He was very discouraged.

In Geisel's opinion, he had a good job. He
created cartoon advertisements for different
products. He also drew cartoons for a few
magazines.

Geisel was skilled at his work, and his advertisements were very successful. But it was not what he really wanted to do for a career. He really wanted to write and illustrate children's books.

He knew he was lucky to be working at all. It was the middle of the Great Depression, and jobs were hard to come by. People with jobs held onto them, even if they didn't like the work. The most important thing was to be working. So Geisel held onto his cartooning jobs. And in his spare time he worked on a children's book.

Geisel had been visiting book publishers in New York City for weeks. He had a manuscript and illustrations for a children's story with him. He had been sure that at least one publisher would want to publish it.

But Geisel already had shown his book to forty-three publishers. Not one of them wanted to publish his story. Many of them thought his story had too much foolishness in it.

Geisel was seldom discouraged. But this was the second book he had written. No one had wanted to publish the first one either. As he walked down the street that day, he decided to give up on writing. He even thought about burning the story in his fireplace!

Suddenly, he heard someone call his name.

"Ted! Ted Geisel!"

It was a man named Mike McClintock. Geisel had gone to college with him.

"What are you doing here, Ted?" his friend
asked. Geisel told him about the book and that
no one wanted to publish it. McClintock saw how
discouraged he was.

"Come to my office," McClintock said. "Let's take a look at it." He explained that he had just started work at a publishing company.

Mike and the other editors liked the story and Ted's drawings. They decided to publish the book.

Ted tried out many titles for the book. He decided to call it *And to Think That I Saw It on Mulberry Street*.

He also decided to use a pen name instead of his real name. He called himself "Dr. Seuss." Seuss was his middle name, and his mother's last name before she was married.

That first Dr. Seuss book was a critical success. Book critics loved it!

Book critics are people who spend a lot of time reading many books. Their opinions are important. The critics who read Dr. Seuss's book were impressed with his talent. They continued to be impressed throughout his long career.

Dr. Seuss's full name was Theodor Seuss Geisel. But his family always called him Ted. He was born in Springfield, Massachusetts, on March 2, 1904.

Geisel's father had several jobs when Geisel was growing up. The most interesting one was zookeeper! Geisel was fascinated by the zoo and would visit his father and the animals often. He began drawing funny, odd-looking creatures at an early age.

But even though Geisel was always doodling in his school notebooks, he didn't think about being an artist.

Geisel attended Dartmouth College in New Hampshire. After he graduated from college, he went to England to study literature at Oxford University. He planned on being a college professor.

But even at Oxford he continued to draw. One day another student, Helen Palmer, saw his drawings. After class she told him he ought to be an artist. They became friends.

Eventually Ted and Helen were married.

Like many writers and artists, Dr. Seuss was very critical of his own work. He worked for months on every story. He would rewrite the story and change the drawings many times.

He also relied on Helen's opinion. She read his stories as he worked on them, and made critical notes.

Most of Dr. Seuss's life was spent as a writer. But he had other careers too. He was also a cartoonist. Some of his cartoons were used for magazine covers. Some expressed his opinions about world events. He also had a successful career as an advertising artist, drawing cartoons for newspaper and magazine advertisements.

During World War II, Ted stopped being Dr. Seuss. He became Captain Ted Geisel. He served his country, as did many other men and women. But even in wartime, he was able to use his creativity. He joined a group of soldiers who made training movies for people who were drafted into the army.

He also created a cartoon character called Gerald McBoing-Boing, who became very popular. Geisel went on to win two Academy Awards for his film work.

After the war, Ted went back to being
Dr. Seuss. He and Helen bought a house near
San Diego, California. It had a tall watchtower.
They built his studio at the top of the tower.

Dr. Seuss worked in his studio for eight
hours every day. He wanted each book to be the
best that it could possibly be.

Where did Dr. Seuss get ideas for his books? Like most creative people, his ideas often came from ordinary things he saw around him.

One day he left a window open near his drawing table. A gust of wind blew one of his drawings of an elephant. The picture landed on top of a drawing of a tree. The elephant seemed to be sitting in the tree.

"Why would an elephant be sitting in a tree?" he wondered.

He gave the idea a great deal of thought.

Eventually he answered the question by writing *Horton Hatches the Egg*.

Many of his books came from his observations of everyday things. But not all of them started out that way.

In 1954, *Life* magazine ran a story about illiteracy among school children. The story said that many children couldn't read because children's books were not interesting enough. In response to this, a publisher asked Dr. Seuss to write a reading book for small children. The publisher made a list of 250 words and explained that these were the most important words for new readers to learn. He told Dr. Seuss that his book could use only those words on the list.

It was difficult work and Dr. Seuss almost gave up. Finally he decided that the first two rhyming words he found would be in the title of the book. He found "cat" and then "hat." And then he had the title, *The Cat in the Hat*. Now all he had to do was write a book to go along with it!

After a year of work, Dr. Seuss finally finished his story. And he had used only 220 different words—even fewer words than he was allowed.

Dr. Seuss had enjoyed the tremendous challenge of writing a book with words for new readers. So, after *The Cat in the Hat* was published, Dr. Seuss wanted to continue to help children learn to read.

He and his wife and some friends started their own publishing company. They called it Beginner Books. Their company published Dr. Seuss's books and also books written by other authors. He helped choose which books to publish and also helped other writers.

This meant that Dr. Seuss now had four careers. He was a writer, an artist, an editor, and a publisher.

In 1960, Dr. Seuss was playing chess with a friend. The friend challenged Dr. Seuss to write a book using only fifty different words.

Dr. Seuss went to work. The result was his most popular book of all, *Green Eggs and Ham*.

Many critics said *Green Eggs and Ham* was the best Dr. Seuss book ever. In a survey that year, six of the best children's books were Dr. Seuss books.

As he grew older, Dr. Seuss had to go to the doctor more frequently. And sitting in waiting rooms was boring. So Dr. Seuss began to do what he did best. He drew while he waited. He wrote a story to go with the drawings. Soon he had written a book for adults called *You're Only Old Once!*

In 1984, Dr. Seuss was awarded the Pulitzer Prize for his work in children's literature. It was a great honor.

Dr. Seuss never retired and never ran out of ideas. His last book, *Oh, the Places You'll Go!* was published when he was eighty-six years old. It turned out to be as popular with college students as it was with children!

Dr. Seuss died on September 24th, 1991. In his long career he did many things. He was a cartoonist, an advertising artist, a movie maker, an author, an editor, and a publisher. He wrote forty-six books that have sold over two hundred million copies.

Dr. Seuss had accomplished a great deal by the time he died. He had spent his life helping children learn to read. And he proved to the world that words are fun and that reading is an enjoyable pastime.

On the day Dr. Seuss died, one young artist drew a special cartoon. In it a small character says sadly that "Dr. Seuss is gone forever." But the character begins to read *The Cat in the Hat*. Then he says, "Dr. Seuss is here forever."

And he *will* be here forever, so long as there are Dr. Seuss books for children of all ages to discover. His books are still as popular as ever. They are in stores and libraries throughout the world. Whenever you're in the mood for some enjoyable reading and especially a good, old-fashioned laugh, check one out!